A CROWN OF GLORY

UGOCHI B. AKINMOLADUN

XUON PRESS

A
CROWN
OF GLORY

UGOCHI B. AKINMOLADUN

XUON PRESS

Xulon Press
2301 Lucien Way #415
Maitland, FL 32751
407.339.4217
www.xulonpress.com

Paperback ISBN-13: 978-1-66286-844-3
Ebook ISBN-13: 978-1-66286-845-0

ACKNOWLEDGEMENTS

I COULD NOT have undertaken this journey without the help of God. I dedicate this book to the Almighty God who has been my source of inspiration and strength. He revealed the title of the book to me in a dream, and gave me the knowledge to write. I am extremely grateful to Him for His endless love, grace, peace, and mercy. I would like to thank my parents for their great love and prayers, especially my late father, Sunday Umere, who taught me how to write when I was younger. He inspired me in many ways. I am really thankful to my siblings for their encouragement and motivation. My warmest appreciation to all the members of RCCG Restoration Villa, Queens, New York, and Dover Assembly, Delaware, for their constant support and prayers. I would like to express my deepest gratitude to my wonderful children for their words of encouragement, support, and inspiration. Of course, my deepest appreciation goes to my amazing husband, Dr. Francis Akinmoladun, for his unconditional love, encouragement, and guidance from the beginning of this project to completion. Also, I wish to extend my special thanks to everyone who has provided me with helpful resources toward the progress of this project. This effort would not have been accomplished without your support. The Lord will reward you all greatly, in Jesus's name.

To everyone reading this book: God's glory will be evident in your life, in Jesus's name. Amen!

FOREWORD

WE GIVE GOD all the Glory for making it possible for the publication of this book. My prayer is that it will be a blessing to all who will find it useful either in counseling or reading for pleasure and buy it as a gift for others.

The author has sauced this book with many relevant scripture passages. She has so only addressed the problem as a woman. This book is aimed at informing the readers of the challenges that women face in life.

The challenges either make you victorious as a child of God or defeat you if you are not on the Lord's side.

Hannah's name means "grace, mercy" in all these challenges. Hannah carries the Grace of God. His Grace was sufficient for her throughout all the years. The story of Hannah is found in 1 Samuel 1- 2.

Hannah demonstrated abounding, constant and steadfast faith in God. Her persistent and passionate prayer lifestyle is commendable. She is heavenly-minded and a promise keeper.

At a time when God needed a trustworthy priest for the people of Israel. Hannah made a vow to give the baby back to God. So, God was in need of a priest, and Hannah was in need of a baby boy. God answered Hannah & Hannah fulfilled her promise to God. It is with humility that I present this book to the readers and counselors believing that it will be a blessing to all.

Sister Grace Oladeru
Destiny Sanctuary- RCCG
Queens, NY

INTRODUCTION

HAVE YOU EVER seen a house maid becoming a queen overnight? This *is* possible! Everyone you come across in life has something to share. Life is full of both sweet and bitter stories. Challenges make you stronger and smarter; without challenges, you cannot move forward. Every problem you overcome takes you to the next level of your journey in life. Often times, the attitude shown during hard times determines the outcomes. We all encounter challenges at certain points in life, but the ability to maintain a positive behavior in the midst of the storms is essential. In fact, creating a positive mindset in difficult times contributes to your well-being. Meditating on God's Word gives you peace and assurance that what you are going through at the moment is not compared to what God has in store for you. The word of God says in Proverbs 3: 5-6, "Trust in the Lord with all your heart, and lean not on your own understanding. [6] In all your ways acknowledge Him, and He shall direct your paths." When going through tough times in life, it is very important to depend on God and not on the situations. Trusting God in times of trouble means we are asking Him to take over because we have no solution to the problems, but He knows the beginning and ending of every problem we face in life. Count it all joy when going through pain because your Father in Heaven is always there to see you through it. God always wants to get involved in everything we do, if we allow Him to. This led me to study the history of a faithful woman in the Bible who went through infertility and pain, but did not let her predicaments stop her from serving and worshipping God.1 Sam 1;2-28. She is an expression of God's grace: A woman of faith and patience, a woman of strength and peace, a woman of honor and great personality, a personality to be emulated. Her life's story is an encouragement to everyone facing the storms of life today. Hannah is a perfect example of a woman of faith in the Bible. Her glory was hidden in her story.

If she could overcome real-life struggles, so can you!

As you read this book, may it bring out the hidden power bestowed on you through the Holy Spirit, and release the grace to overcome every challenge you encounter in life, in Jesus's name. Amen!

Chapter One
GRACE PERSONIFIED

GRACE IS A gift from God to everyone He created. He gives it generously to mankind; it is unmerited. The grace of God in Hannah's life is a special kind of grace. She is clothed with a saving grace that reveals her personality. She is a completely quiet woman who understands the power of grace that works inside of her. She is kind, respectful, tolerant, honest, and courageous. Everything about her reflects grace. Hannah practices and demonstrates the power of grace daily. Despite her struggling, she chooses to interact with people around her with respect. Even though her environment is not encouraging, she prefers to stay happy. She does not transfer her sorrow to people; instead, she turns it into worship. (1 Sam. 1: 10). Her desires and beliefs are to serve God. She enjoys going to Shiloh to pour out her burdens to the Lord because she believes that God is greater than her present situation. The grace of God is so powerful in her life that even in the midst of trials, it sustains her. She allows the grace of God to work through her heart with peace, courage, strength, and hope. She ensures that the grace of God in her life is not misused. She lives her life to please God. She strongly trusts the power of God with all her life. The quality of being worthy of honor and respect is inside of her. All this contributes to her personality. Finally, God honored her patience. Grace takes her to the throne of honor. She is decorated and beautified with grace and honor. Her life is the expression of God's grace.

The life of Hannah simplifies grace that is worthy of being emulated. In today's dispensation, a lot of people are operating without the grace of God; some do not understand the meaning of grace, and others misuse the grace of God. Human beings are created to walk according to the will of God, but the case is different because they have chosen to be impatient with God, especially when they are faced with the challenges of life. People tend to forget that the grace of God can do the impossible. They forget to worship and pray more in times of challenges, and instead, they give power to their situations. They give excuses as to why they cannot go to a place of worship to pray. Hannah shows a great example of a woman who carries grace without doubt. She goes to Shiloh every year to worship God with her shame.1 Sam. 1:9-10 She believes in the power of grace to deliver her from her predicament. In the scripture, when Paul asked God to take his ailment away so he would be able to serve God more efficiently, God says in 2 Corinthians 12:9, " **My grace is sufficient for you, for my strength is made perfect in weakness.**" This means that the grace of God is adequate for all. He turns our weaknesses, sicknesses, sorrows, shame, inabilities, to perfect. He wants His children to rely on Him because He has our lives in His hands.

Often, people wonder why they go through hardships, even when they believe in God. I have heard people say things like, "But we pray to God; we believe in God; we go to a place of worship. Our lives still remain the same."

I have seen some people stop going to a place of worship because they did not receive what they expected from God at the moment. Many times, we focus on our own suffering, instead of focusing on the One who knows the genesis and end of our difficulties. We place our pains over the "God of All Impossibilities." Sometimes, God makes us wait to see if we would present our burdens to Him or change our ways of life. Also, He wants us to wait at the appropriate time to deliver us. He knows what He is going to release to us might not work perfectly well with our present capacity. He knows our yesterday, today, and tomorrow. He knows our ability to handle the things He puts in our care. He knows best what we need at any time. So, He supplies our needs according to His will. Hannah waited patiently, and she was graciously honored. If God is making you wait and wait, do not be in a hurry; do not give up your faith, and do not bargain for less. We do not understand why God is causing us to wait during these painful periods. Hannah did not stop worshipping God, even when God answered her prayers. She kept her faith, and that was why she was able to fully reap her reward. She was blessed beyond her expectations. God has greater plans for you; He has bundles of blessings for you in the future. Every year has its own blessings that God releases unto us. Do not miss the future blessings by quitting to serve God due to today's blessings. God is moved by our service to Him.

Continue walking in grace; let your life showcase grace, and you will never be put to shame.

ACTIVATION PRAYERS

1. Thank you, Lord, for the precious gift of life granted to me every day.
2. Thank you, Lord, for your precious blood over my household.
3. Thank you, Lord, for Your grace and peace in my life, in Jesus's name.
4. Father, give me the grace to serve you in all situations, in Jesus's name.
5. Father, help me to wait patiently for my reward, in Jesus's name.
6. Oh Lord, grant me the grace to make use of your grace in my life, in Jesus's name.

Chapter Two

EXCEPTIONAL LOVE

LOVE IS A deep feeling of affection toward something or someone. There are different types of love that people show to each other. But, the love of God surpasses all. In this chapter, the love that Elkanah — the husband of Hannah — extends to her, will be analyzed briefly. 1 Sam. 1:4-5. Hannah's husband loves her without expectations of getting anything in return. He spreads his love to her, even in her distress. He sees beyond her physical appearance; he sees beyond her present condition; he sees her as a woman full of God's grace and honor. He sees royalty in her. He sees a woman who carries uncommon favor. He is carried away by her uniqueness. He sees a woman who is endowed with God's glory. He sees a mother of kings and queens. He sees her as a woman with great potential, and he adores her. His love for her is beyond what he feels or controls.

This type of love is the highest love a man can spread to his woman. Elkanah has two wives: the second has children for him, but Hannah is still expecting God to answer her supplications at the time. However, she is her husband's favorite. In fact, her husband pays more attention to her than the other wife; he ensures she never worries about anything. He tries to care for all her material and physical needs. To prove his love to her, he emphatically said to her, "Am I not better to you than ten sons?" 1 Sam. 1:8. He says this to make her feel happy. His perspective about her is totally different from how other people see her. But that does not solve her problems (1 Sam. 1:4-5). In spite of all this, Hannah is silently suffering in pain. The joy of every woman is to have children in her husband's house. Every woman deserves the joy of motherhood. No woman deserves to be left out!

Subsequently, Hannah did not allow the love that her husband showers on her make her forget to serve God. She is not serving God only because she is expecting children from God. She serves God because she knows that it is *only* the love of God that can change her story to glory. She believes that the love of God is everlasting. She never stops believing in the ultimate love that washes away sins, and redeems all from evil chains. These days, some people serve God because of what they *want* from God. As soon as they get what they are praying for, they say goodbye to God. God does not think the way we think. Before we act, He knows the beginning, middle, and end of our intentions. Why would you hide from the One who created you? Why would you pretend to love He who is *called* Love.

Many people are being carried away by material things, or how people stretch out love to them by buying them expensive cars and beautiful houses; and, of course, living a luxurious life-style. They do not want to hear you talk about serving God. They would ask questions like: Who is God? Does He exist?

In the case of Hannah, she had it all, but she did not allow those things to interfere in her worship of her Savior. She did not allow the love of her husband to affect her spirituality. Even though she loved her husband dearly, she did not let worldly affection supersede her relationship with God. Instead, she loved God more. Material things will end here, but your soul will not. Serving God with your wealth and achievement enables you to enjoy the peace of mind that comes from above. Hannah knew that the love her husband had for her could not solve her problems, so she never compromised her faith.

What are you doing with your precious time? Are you worshipping God in the midst of trials? How are you protecting the love that people show you? Every day is a brand new day given to us by the Creator, a second chance to be better than the previous day. What we do with the opportunity of each day matters. A person with a great vision of the future plans ahead and trusts God for manifestations. Do not let a day go by without praying, planning, working, and trusting God. Rely on God's power when facing the challenges of life. In the world of distractions and pressure around us today, one could be taken away from communicating with God, the perfect communicator. The best place to protect your wealth or accomplishments is in the hands of God. The more you love serving God, the more He shows you love by blessing you with the peace that will cause you to enjoy life as long as you live. In John 14: 27, the scripture says, **"Peace I leave with, my peace I give to you. Not as the world gives do I give to you. Let not your hearts be troubled. Neither let them be afraid."** God is ever faithful to His word. He knows everything that happens to us on a daily basis. He loves us more than we could imagine. He cares for us and that is why His desire is to give us peace that terminates sorrow, peace that is not sold in the marketplace. Peace that keeps our hearts pure. Peace that calms down the storms of life.

Even though Hannah was deeply loved by her husband, she remained steadfast in the Lord, knowing that her future was in the hands of the Almighty. Her faithfulness spoke for her. Hannah's kind of love shown to God was reflected in her behavior to everyone she came across. This was the love that came from inside of her. She was ornamented with the spirit of love: a godly woman indeed! Elkanah, her husband, saw the golden heart of love that God had deposited in his wife, and that was why he fell into total love with her. She really enjoyed the love of God through her lifetime. Allow God to wear you with the garments of love that attracts special grace. The love you cannot compare to the love of the world, the love that is rich and pure, priceless, and immeasurable. The love that does not discriminate. God's love supersedes the love of the world. Do not let bitterness rule or overwhelm you, but instead, let the love of God control your being.

ACTIVATION PRAYERS

1. Thank you, Jesus, for showing your love to me and my family.
2. My God, create within me, a pure and loving spirit, in Jesus's name.
3. Oh Lord, cause me to enjoy your love all the days of my life, in Jesus's name.
4. Father, make your love in my life attract men to you, in Jesus's name.
5. Father, let your word manifest in my life, in Jesus's name.
6. Father, cover me with your love in Jesus's name

Chapter Three
BITTERNESS AND INFERTILITY

BITTERNESS IS WHEN you are not happy about unpleasant conditions that occur to you or someone close to you. It significantly affects the state of mind of an individual. There are different ways that people experience bitterness. It could be that someone who is dear to them passed away, or someone they are about to marry had an accident and passed. People go through bitterness at a point in life, though it differs. Bitterness can make you feel like the world is full of sorrow and disappointment. It can turn your joyful moments into dismay. The way people handle bitterness is also different. On the other hand, infertility is the inability to conceive and reproduce after several times of sexual intercourse with your spouse. Failure to represent something, duplicate copies, or having babies in a marriage is quite disappointing. For instance, a person who was given a certain amount of money to start a small business is expected to use the sum to make more money and multiply. Unfortunately, some cases are not the same. A woman could get married this month and get pregnant the next month, while another woman could have difficulties in conceiving. Life is full of wonders. In a situation where a woman is battling bitterness and infertility, it can lead to depression and anxiety.

Hannah went through tremendous stress psychologically and emotionally for years. The scripture in 1 Samuel 1:10 states, **"And she was in bitterness of soul, and prayed to the Lord and wept in anguish."** She went through pains and humiliations in her marital home, yet, she never complained or transferred her frustrations to the people around her. She had all the qualities a virtuous woman would have, but still felt bitterness in her soul because she could not reproduce at the time. There is an appointed time for everyone in life. Everybody did not come to this world the same day, so we have different times of manifestations. God has a purpose and specific pattern for everyone. He leads us according to His purpose, because He knows us before we were formed in our mother's wombs. He knows and sees every step we take in life. In fact, He is the architect of our lives. After reading the story of Hannah thoroughly, I deeply understood that her being barren for a while was divinely planned. God is God, no one can question Him for doing what pleases Him. He has reasons for everything He allows to happen. He purposely allowed Hannah to be barren for a while for Him to glorify Himself in her life (1 Sam. 1:5). As a result, He ordered her paths through the period of waiting, and ensured she lived to experience laughter at last. Hannah suffered the embarrassment of not giving birth to children in her husband's house numerous times.

In fact, the humiliations came from someone who shared the same building with her, someone who shared the same husband with her, and someone who knew her. Peninnah, the second wife, insulted her, called her names, and created unnecessary scenes to provoke her spirit.1Sam. 1:6. Instead of responding to her in the same manner, she would cry and went before her God in supplications. Her tears were prayers as well. Imagine you are traveling to another state for an annual convention to pray to God, and someone had intentionally instigating a fight against you to distract you. What would you do? Peninnah tried her possible best to terrorize her, but she stood firm in the Word of God. When you are in a good relationship with God, He controls your mind, and He will not let you stumble and fall. A lot of believers claim to believe in God, but it does not reflect in their behavior. Some believers react very quickly to insults. Some would tell you they cannot stand being humiliated, especially from close associates. The point is that when you are a true believer, you are not in control of yourself anymore; the Holy Spirit operates through you, and takes charge of your life. At times, we act before we react, and we allow flesh to take over before the Holy Spirit. God allows certain things to happen in our lives to prove

Himself. Also, He tests our faith to see if we could stand trials and temptations before He takes us to the next level.

Hannah is quite an expression of a true believer. She permits the Holy Spirit into her life permanently. She lets the Holy Spirit have His way in her life. She does not let her psychological distress affect the way she relates to people. Her ideology of handling distress and humiliation is far beyond ordinary. A believer is expected to show a level of humility in every aspect of life, whether things are going well or not. People face different challenges every day in life, and the way we react to difficulties determines the outcomes. Seeking the will of God first before acting is not enough, but seeking and waiting for His response gives birth to a pleasant ending. As a believer, always ask for the leading of the Holy Spirit to order your paths each day, because every day has its own blessings that are attached to it. Ask for daily guidance and His will for your life will be done.

Hannah overcame her challenges through her faith in God. She committed her suffering into God's hands, and she was not disappointed with the results. She recovered all she thought she had lost in the past, in countless ways. 1 Sam. 1:20. God did not allow her to be put to shame. He took her humiliators, oppressors, and tormentors by surprise. She was crowned with beauty and honor, because she demonstrated a godly character throughout her times of trial.

Do not let bitterness overwhelm you; it has an expiration date!

Irrespective of what you are going through in life, always involve God in it. Allow Him to walk in, and through, you. He is the owner of your destiny. He is more than capable to see you through the good and bad times, if you permit Him. He knew you *before*, He knows you *now*, and will know you *forever*.

ACTIVATION PRAYERS

1. Father, fill me with the Holy Spirit daily, in Jesus's name.
2. Holy Spirit, take over every challenge of my life, in Jesus's name.
3. Father, empower me to overcome every ugly situation opposing my faith, in Jesus's name.
4. My Father, surprise my enemy with your miracle in my life, in Jesus's name.
5. Lord, beautify my family for your name to be glorified, in Jesus's name.

Chapter Four

DIVINE ENCOUNTER

HAVE YOU EVER met a drug addict who later became a global evangelist or have you seen a person born crippled who started walking after thirty-five years of age? Incredible things happen in people's lives daily. God is amazing for doing amazing things. People marvel with miracles they come across in life. "Divine" is associated with God. It has to do with the spiritual, heavenly, and holy. A divine encounter is an extraordinary manifestation of the power of God orchestrated to bring honor to the Almighty. A divine encounter is an unpredicted visitation that transforms lives. A divine encounter is an extreme manifestation of the power of God to bring honor to His mighty name. It is a visitation that is designed in such a way that is beyond human understanding. Nobody can explain the outcomes of a divine encounter. God works in a marvelous way, and no one can understand His intentions. He made all things by Himself, this means that humans are divinely created. The original purpose of God creating humans is to walk according to His plans. A divine encounter occurs when a person has a relationship with God. It is an occurrence that changes the life of an individual from despair to encouragement. It is a contact that turns impossibilities to possibilities, barrenness to fruitfulness, sorrow to laughter, disappointment to appointment, natural to supernatural, and ordinary to extraordinary. It is an experience that is beyond human comprehension. The Word of God manifests in our lives every day. God uses His mighty power to fulfill His purpose in our lives. He is continually working in the lives of individuals to make Himself known to the world. He performed wonders in the days of old; He performs wonders today, and will still perform wonders in the future. He also reveals His wonders to those who work to be closer to Him. He is God all by Himself, the Uncreated Creator, and unlimited God.

Hannah was a devoted woman of God, who honored God all through her lifetime. Even though she was suffering and in a deep pain, she did not compromise her faith. She had been going to Shiloh for years, in 1 Sam. 1:7, praying and expecting God for a miracle, but it seemed like answers were not coming. She insisted that serving God was what she had chosen to do, her honor for God was deeper than her situation. She strongly believed in the God of all impossibilities, and she believed that her prayers would be answered someday. She believed that her agony would be taken away, and she believed that weeping may last in the night, but joy comes in the morning. She loved God with all her heart. The scripture says that, "**All things work together for good to them that love God, to them who are the called according to His purpose,**" (Rom. 8:28). For every challenge in life, there is always a breakthrough. God has a way of making things happen in order to bring glory to Himself. His time is different from our time. His time for humanity is perfect timing. He never let His people down. He cares so much about them that He keeps watching over them. He is the beginning and the ending, the Alpha and the Omega. He knows and sees every single pain we go through in life. He is a God of perfection, and He does whatever He says, as people who are called according to God's purpose are required to love and trust Him in all circumstances. Loving and trusting God for who He is makes a significant difference in the lives of individuals. His response to such people is rewarding. He rewards with a mind-blowing blessing. Whatever you face in the journey of life, it has a purpose and timing. Hannah went through her times of trial with confidence because she knew her purpose in life. Everything in life has a time and purpose for manifestations. In the scripture, it says, "**To everything there is a season, and a time to every purpose under the heaven,**" (Eccles. 3:1). The question is, what are your reactions when going through trials? If you are going through hard times, do not lose hope, stay strong and focus on God. He is the only one who can create and recreate the things He created. He has the power to do all things. He is more than capable of taking you out of difficult situations and wrapping you in a garment of everlasting joy. He is with you always. Also, reminiscing about what He has done in the past helps to reaffirm your faith that He will deliver you. Always apply the proper application toward any condition you find yourself in life. Trust and obey God's commandment, and serve Him with all your heart.

The divine encounter is an amazing power of God, and it changes life. Hannah went to Shiloh every year to worship the Lord, and Eli never noticed her. Apparently, a lot of people do visit Shiloh every year, so he could not know or identify everyone. However, on this particular day, something miraculous happened. Hannah was in deep pain, and bitterly weeping and praying to God. She was pouring out her shame, sorrow, pains, dejection, depression, sadness, suffering, and agony to the only One who could save her. She was tired of experiencing humiliation and oppression in her matrimonial home. She was tired of being bullied and the name-calling. She cried tirelessly and deeply prayed within her soul, because she understood the power of prayer. In her prayer, she made a promise to God. Her prayers touched God and divine arrangements commenced. The spirit of God started working through Eli for her deliverance. Immediately, Eli noticed her and asked her, **"How long will you be drunk, put your wine away from you?" (1 Sam. 1: 14).** God always uses people to carry out His assignments (Gal. 4:4). He used Eli to deliver Hannah from shame. When the appointed time of an individual comes, it accomplishes the goal. It cannot fail, and nothing can stop it from manifesting. If you are waiting, please wait for the appointed time; it will surely come.

Moreso, Hannah's response to Eli indicates the kind of woman she was. She was full of grace, humility, and honor. She demonstrated her strong belief through her humility. She did not react negatively when being accused or provoked. She told him that she was just an ordinary woman who was experiencing deep pain and anguish. She did not drink alcohol not alone being drunk; she was only communicating and pouring out her heart, in great sorrow, to God. Eli answered and told her to go in peace, that the Lord had heard her supplications. Divine arrangement activated!

When we are going through pain or sorrow in life, it is the *best* time to go to God in prayer. Sometimes, it can be difficult, but it is the right time to do it. It is not the time to complain or transfer frustrations to people around you; it is not the time to call family and friends to expose your conditions to them. It is a period to trust God's power and love for you. It is a time to pray and believe in the God who takes burdens away. The Lord really wants us to express our troubles to Him in faith. Hannah genuinely poured out her worries and pains to God, and He wiped away her shame. God can use anyone as a mediator to help us in life. Eli was the one God used to answer her prayers. Subsequently, he was praying for her; he stood in the gap for her, interceding for her. I call such a person a destiny helper! Always be aware of the people that come across us in life. God uses anybody to be a destiny helper. The ability to respond to every situation in an appropriate manner comes with favor. In the case of Hannah, she was going through physical, psychological, and social problems that could have affected her emotions, but she did not allow them to affect her. Instead, she responded honorably to every provoked question or abuse that came her way. This was one of the reasons she was significantly favored and honored. She gained a very high integrity in the sight of God and man. Her goals in life were to please her Maker, and make peace with everyone. She had more than enough that she was battling with, and she did not want to add unnecessary stress to it. The ability to tolerate unpleasant conditions for a long period of time without reacting to ugly situations involves great qualities. Enduring difficulties, stress, and trials in order to achieve greatness in life is rewarding. Hannah endured pains, and she was rewarded beyond human comprehension.

In addition, Hannah's cry touched God, and He came down with His power and glory to prove Himself mighty in her life. After the encounter, Hannah's life was not the same. Her physiological and mental health changed. She believed something great had happened in her life. She trusted in the power that rested on her; she knew the sound of joy was about to be heard in her home. She believed that the God of "impossibilities" had visited her, and she knew that the visit to Shiloh that year was unusual. She saw a miracle coming her way.1 Sam.1:17-18. Her visit to Shiloh that year was not in vain; it led to her throne of honor. She did not miss her divine encounter. Whatever you go through in life, always submit yourself to your Creator, who knows the source of all problems and solutions. He cares for you more than you do for yourself. Believe in His saving name, and He will deliver you. Always be conscious of yourself and your environment so you don't miss your destiny helpers. For every challenge you face in life, there is always a person God has assigned to help you out. Watch out, so you don't miss your destiny lifter. Do not allow bitterness to rule or overwhelm you; it is not going to last for a long time. It has an expiration date!

ACTIVATION PRAYERS

1. 1. I'm grateful to God for my life and family.
2. 2. Thank you, Lord, for your unfailing grace in my family.
3. 3. Father, please grant me the grace to pursue peace always.
4. 4. Father, let your Spirit lead me through every situation of life.
5. 5. Oh Lord, don't let me wait on you in vain.
6. 6. Father, deliver me from every shame and sorrow.
7. 7. Father, help me not to miss my day of divine encounter.

Chapter Five
THE VOW

A VOW IS a promise made by an individual toward a specific something without expecting anything in return. It is a sacrificial giving. It could be that someone makes a vow by sacrificing his or her time, talents, finances, services, prayers, worship, or praise to God. A vow is a promise that has a great effect in your life. Every vow you make comes from a sincere heart, and is expected to be fulfilled. Often times, people vow when they are going through difficult times, and as soon as they are out of it, they forget their promise. I have seen people make vows to serve God with their talents; they are dedicated to the things of God when they need God's intervention in their lives. However, when God changes their situations from suffering into flourishing, they stop serving Him, they forget their days of sorrow, they forget the Most powerful God who brought them out of bondage. They give excuses as to why they are not available to serve God the way they used to. Some turn their backs on the things of the Lord because they believe their problems are solved, and they can now live the life they want. They forget their promises. The scripture says, "When you make a vow to God, do not delay to fulfill it. He has no pleasure in fools; fulfill your vow," (Eccl. 5:4).

When you make a promise to God, and when you are hoping for something, fulfill your vows. When God answers your prayers, keep serving Him, and you will get more blessings from Him. In the case of Hannah, she made a vow, fulfilled it, and never stopped serving God. In fact, she sacrifices all her life to God. Serving God with everything He has given is allowing His blessings to run after you. Whatever you sacrifice pays off in due season, so don't stop vowing, don't stop fulfilling, and don't stop serving God. When we honor God with our sacrifices, He receives them and pours down His blessings to us. Sacrificing your time to God is *not* a waste. In fact, you gain a lot from Him, because all blessings come from above. Vowing to God draws you nearer to Him. It is a time to communicate the reasons why you are making such a commitment. He wants to hear verbally from you. It is a decision you make and must be determined to fulfill it. So, it motivates you to work toward your targets; the more you dedicate your time working hard to get it done, the closer you are communicating with God. Vowing draws you closer to God because the attachment is toward what you ask God to do for you.

Hannah is a woman of integrity and character. She is truly an embodiment of God's grace. She has great qualities that make her stands out among others. Everyone's perspective and projection to religion is different. Some people have "being giving" as a quality, while some have patience as a quality, and others have teaching as a quality. Hannah had distinctive qualities that differentiated her from other godly women in the Bible. She served the Lord with her whole heart. To be sincere, she had good characters to be emulated. Hannah made a vow to God, and said that if He could turn her barrenness to fruitfulness, her garment of shame to honor, her sorrow to laughter, weeping to joy, suffering to peace, agony to rejoicing, humiliation to admiration, then she would sacrifice her unborn child to Him. She knew what she wanted at the time and was very specific (1 Sam. 1:12) Hannah had been going to Shiloh for many years; she had been praising, worshipping, and praying to God, and nothing happened, but then she tried a vow. She kept trying different ways to please God, without doubting the power of God. She spoke to God about her vow. She was a woman of faith.

Many times, we get tired of serving God because we are not getting what we request, or it seems our prayers are not answered. In a situation where everything seems impossible, that is the moment we need to change our strategies. If you try worship, praise, and prayers, and answers are not coming, try making a vow. Provoke the power of God with a vow. Make a promise that sounds impossible to yourself. Challenge God with your vow. In Numbers 21: 2-3, when Israel was faced with challenges, he did not pray;

he made a vow, and God answered him immediately. There is a place of praise, worship, and prayer.

If you have a good relationship with God, you understand how to relate to Him appropriately. God knows our thoughts and our intentions. He knows whether we are going to fulfill our vows or not, so He works with us accordingly. Hannah meant it when she said she would give back her child to God. He sees her heart, and granted her request. She specifically asked for a male child and did not doubt the Almighty God, who can change a hopeless story into a glorious one. Be specific in your request, and believe that your requests are met. God is not a man, that He should lie; He does everything He says. He can reciprocate what He has done in the past because He lives in the past, present, and future. He can do all things. He is the author of our lives.

Furthermore, Hannah was a committed and determined woman. She fixed her eyes on God and did not allow the noise outside in the world to distract her attention. She was observant and filled with the Holy Spirit. Her mode of communication attracted favor to her life. The Holy Spirit was working, leading, directing, and watching her. She was controlled by the Spirit of God. Her life was predestined by God; everything happened to her for a purpose. The journey of her faith led her to the throne of honor prepared for her. In life, people go through what they never planned, for not knowing that God has everything concerning them planned out even before they were born (Jer. 1-5). When you are going through tough times, remember that you are not alone; God is always with you; promise Him something that you will do when He answers you, and keep your faith high. Adopt a positive attitude; be conscious of what you do or say, and patiently wait for God's plan to manifest. He knows you more than you know yourself, and He can do much more for you as long as you are working according to His instructions. Hannah's vow changed her condition for good. She gave back to God the child she had been waiting for. She fulfilled her promise to God. As a result, the God of "impossibilities" added sweetness to her bitterness. He performed a miracle in the life of a barren woman. God is an amazing God; nobody can understand His Wisdom. He makes great things out of nothing. I call Him the God of Wonders! Try Him with your vow today, and watch Him transform your life for the best.

ACTIVATION PRAYERS

1. Thank you, Lord, for your blessings in my family.
2. Thank you, Lord, for the grace to serve you.
3. Father, fill me with the spirit of patience and endurance.
4. Father, change my story for good, in Jesus's name.
5. Oh Lord, turn my weeping into laughter, in Jesus's name.
6. Lord, let Your wonders reflect in my family.

Chapter Six
GLORY REVEALED

THE GLORY OF God is something no one can define. It is far beyond human understanding. It is impossible to describe it. Psalm 19:1 says, **"The Heavens declare the glory of God, and the firmament shows His handiwork." The** Heavens honor and revere God's glory. The glory of God is the infinite greatness, magnificent beauty, and Spirit of God. Glory is the splendor of God, the praise or worship rendered to God. God reveals His glory to humanity every day. His glory is what we see on a daily basis; His glory surrounds the earth. The first time I traveled by air, I looked out the plane window and was marveled. The view was so beautiful and marvelous. Seeing the magnificent mountains, clouds, and seas that God created was glorious. I thought of how great and mighty the glory of God was. I imagined how all of these beautiful creatures came into existence with simply a spoken word. I thought of the greatness of God; words could not express the wonders of God because it was beyond my utmost understanding. I could not say a word, but worship and revere the Most High God. From that moment, my understanding of the glory of God changed. His glory is everywhere, but nobody can comprehend it. It is indescribable. When the glory of God descends upon an individual, it transforms the life of the person. Every human being is a creature of God's glory. Everyone is created with a unique glory. Apart from the physical glory that we can see, there is a concealed glory that God deposited in the life of everyone, and He is the only One who can reveal it. The glory of Hannah was hidden in her story. It was not made clear to the people living with her. Hannah believed that God had great plans for her, and she did not give up. She knew that one day her conditions would change for good. She strongly believed in the power and glory of God. Hannah humbled herself in everything she did. She believed that God answered prayers, and trusted God for His infinite glory, knowing that, with God, nothing was impossible. Her love for God was authentic. Even in the storm, her faith was stronger, and her eyes were fixed on the only One who can do all things. The glory of the Lord that was kept away from the world was clearly known to her and her loving husband when she conceived. Later, the whole world testified about the glory of God she carried. The Lord decorated her with glory, and it was revealed.

Hannah's crown of glory was waiting for her at the appointed time. The reward was full of the wonders of God. The ability to patiently wait for her crown was predestined. Everything that happened to her during her trying times was orchestrated by God. When the time God wanted to showcase His glory through her came, the whole world heard about her. Psalm 102:13 states that, "Thou shalt arise and have mercy upon Zion, for the time to favor her, yea, the set time, is come." When the set time of Hannah came, God arose and showed her mercy. The glory of God manifested in her life. Her appointed time had come. Her period of waiting was over. God made her laugh and He lifted her above her enemies. 1 Sam 2:1.When the set time of a person comes, nothing can stop it. When God desires to favor an individual, no power can stop Him. When He desires to visit a person, even that person cannot prevent Him because He is the Chief Controller of everything. Time and seasons are in His hands. He fails not. Hannah was graced to shine her light and her life was decorated with grace. If you are going through tough times at the moment, face it with faith that you are an overcomer. Always see yourself as a winner, not a loser. Encourage yourself with the Word of God in Jeremiah 29: 1. You are created by the only One who has your life in His hand. He has ordained you before you were born. Your situation does not move Him; He works by His time. He is watching over you to ensure you fulfill the purpose you are ordained for. Your attitude when facing life's challenges matters. Your perception regarding the current situation has a great effect on the outcome. Don't focus your attention on the problems; fix your eyes on God and be prayerful like Hannah.

He is working in your favor; He knows the perfect time to release blessings for you. Hannah kept serving and obeying God, not knowing that He kept records of her good attitudes. While she was pleasing God, He had already favored her according to a specific time. God's timing is far different than ours. In Ecclesiastes 3:1, the Word of God says, **"To everything there is a season, and a time to every purpose under the heaven."** She was beautified with glory. The light of the world lit up her light and changed her story to glory. He turned her condition of bitterness into sweetness. She patiently and majestically emerged onto her throne of honor, in the presence of her mockers. People who called her barren, now called her blessed.

Have you been humiliated in the past, or are you facing humiliation right now? Are people calling you all sorts of names because of your predicament? Don't respond to them; don't change who you are. Don't occupy your mind with things that are irrelevant to your destiny. Instead, use it as a motivation to strive against all odds. God is interested in changing your story to glory. Are you willing to serve Him for the rest of your life? Make up your mind to let Him into your life today, and you will forever be a victor. Despite all Hannah went through, she did not stop worshipping and trusting God with her situation, and at the end of it all, she was crowned with honor. She was lifted above her sorrowful conditions and her tears were wiped away.

Hannah asked God for a child. He gave her *children*. He answered her prayers and blessed her with wonderful three sons and two daughters. 2 Sam. 2:21. He crowned her with the garment of honor and glory. The purpose of God for her life manifested at the perfect timing. She trusted in the Lord and waited for her time of glory to manifest, and it came to pass. Hannah majestically emerged on the throne of honor in the presence of her mockers. She praised the Lord who answered her prayers. She recognized and acknowledged the lifter of her head. Her time of celebration had finally arrived. Her mouth was filled with songs of victory, songs of overcoming. God proved to the world that He was a God of glory. Whatever it is that you are going through at the moment, put your trust in God, and wait on His time. Do not give up on God. Your appointed time will certainly speak for itself. If Hannah could overcome, you can overcome any obstacles that come your way.

ACTIVATION PRAYERS

1. I appreciate the Lord for His grace and mercy over my family.
2. Thank you, Lord, for your blessings on my family,
3. Father, decorate my life with your grace.
4. Father, manifest your glory in my family.
5. Father, let everything you deposited in my family begin to manifest, in Jesus's name.

"He raises the poor from the dust and lifts the beggar from the ash heap, to set them among princes and make them inherit the throne of glory. For the pillars of the earth are the Lord's, and He has set the world upon them."

1 Samuel 2